MW01005967

Rethinking Church
A Guide for the Perplexed and Disillusioned

Ron Highfield

Keledei
PUBLICATIONS

An Imprint of Sulis International Press
Los Angeles | Dallas | London

RETHINKING CHURCH: A GUIDE FOR THE PERPLEXED
AND DISILLUSIONED
Copyright ©2021 by Ron Highfield. All rights reserved.

All Scripture quotations, unless otherwise indicated, are taken from
the Holy Bible, New International Version®, NIV®. Copyright
©1973, 1978, 1984, 2011 by Biblica, Inc.™ Used by permission of
Zondervan. All rights reserved. www.zondervan.com The "NIV"
and "New International Version" are trademarks registered in the
United States Patent and Trademark Office by Biblica, Inc.™

Cover design by Sulis International Press.
Photo by Pawan Sharma

ISBN (print): 978-1-946849-90-8
ISBN (eBook): 978-1-946849-88-5

Published by Keledei Publications
An Imprint of Sulis International
Los Angeles | Dallas | London

www.sulisinternational.com

Contents

Foreword

American churches are beset _(threatened)_ by woes on every side. The older generation, those who formed the core of yesterday's congregations, now often feel like strangers in their own households. The whole practice of "doing church" as it is conducted now seems foreign to them— the public worship, the organization, the "brand enhancement" and the breathless proliferation _(growth)_ of "programs" have produced in them a greater and greater sense of alienation. A sense of responsibility, and perhaps sheer habit, drive them to remain in the fellowship, but much of the joy has essentially faded.

In the meantime, the younger generation, often "spiritual" but theologically and biblically illiterate, and at the same time pressed and impressed by a culture which has not only ceased to see the churches as something positive, but even as worthless or regressive, increasingly find themselves in a similar dilemma. While the older generation feels that the church has been so transformed that it no longer seems relevant to their lives, the younger generation has accepted the culture's verdict that church is not only no longer necessary but is even a counter-productive force, standing in the way of true progress. In this at least the old and the young agree: Something seems wrong with the way we do church.

Some churches react to this dilemma by retreating into a fortress mentality, holding on to tradition by the fingernails, discouraged by dwindling numbers and general despair. They set up a defensive line against change, all the while nevertheless fading away—slowly but surely. Other churches resort to rather desperate attempts at customer satisfaction, seeking to give potential attendees whatever the culture or the polls say they want. The latter approach sometimes leads to spectacular "success" in the form of massive attendance at carefully-crafted, audience-directed "worship experiences." But this approach is often followed closely by an increasing need for larger bureaucracies and larger budgets.

Ron Highfield calls for another, much more revolutionary way to meet these challenges. He joins Jesus in suggesting that it is unwise to put new wine in old wineskins. Tinkering with superficial changes to the present practice of "church" will not get the job done— whether the tinkering comes from the Right or the Left. What is needed, he suggests, is a return to the simple, original ideas of Jesus and his earliest disciples about what the Church is, and what it is not, what it *may* do, and what it *must* do. Too often, he says, what it is doing is not essential to its being. Its true nature and purpose have disappeared into an immensely distracting cacophony of budgets, staffs, real estate, strategic plans, and public spectacles. The resulting tumult has begotten the worship wars; battles over church and state issues; distress over the gradual loss of "prerogatives", etc. These distractions find their origins in this misdirection, not from the essence of what the church is, or what authentic Christian corporate life ought to be.

Ron's message may be hard for some to hear. Many churches which fancy themselves as "progressive" feel they are thereby radical reformers. But these same churches may find themselves uncomfortable with real reform—based on going back to square one and re-thinking the whole enterprise. The particular wineskin they have been using simply cannot be filled with new wine without expecting a disastrous explosion. What may be required may also be too onerous to bear? Jobs, after all, are at stake; not to mention looming mortgage payments.

Can you think of a church without a staff, without a building, without a budget, as a church in full flower, unencumbered and able to center on the actual mission to which it was called? Or are you more inclined to think of this kind of church as no more than a tiny bud, not yet opened up to its "potential" until it has developed into an attention getting, spectacular, multimillion dollar enterprise? Read this book, and then see how you wish to answer this question.

John F. Wilson
Emeritus Dean and Professor of Religion
Seaver College
Pepperdine University

Preface

Rethinking Church arises out of my struggle to understand the place of the church in the world and my relationship to it. I wrote to clarify my thinking and help others to similar clarity. It is not a comprehensive study of the doctrine and history of the church. I do not use jargon or footnotes, and I do not engage in debate with other authors. There are plenty of big books about the church; we do not need another. I wanted to write a short book that anyone can read in two or three hours without using a dictionary. The argument appeals to the Bible and the reader's experience with churches. I do not ask you to trust my knowledge of obscure sources. You already have all the information you need to make your own judgment.

Like many of you, I do not remember a time I was not held within the embrace of the church. She was to me mother, teacher, and guardian. She taught me about creation, Abraham, Daniel, and Jesus. And I loved her for it. From early childhood onward, I felt a call to ministry. After some hesitancy, I listened to that call, got the required training, and served churches for eight years in preaching, youth, and college ministry. After completing my Ph.D., I began teaching theology at a major Christian university and serving in leadership roles in local churches. Except as a small child, I do not think I was ever naïve about the weaknesses and sins of the people that comprise the church. Nevertheless, I hoped that strong leadership and good teaching could help the church do great things.

About ten years ago, after many frustrating attempts to simplify church life and bring it more into line with the simple New Testament vision, I began to realize that the structures, ingrained expectations, and traditions that guided the church would neutralize any effort at systemic reform. I tried to make peace with this situation and resign myself to working within an imperfect system to achieve some good. However, about five years ago, I began to entertain the idea that the traditional way churches organize themselves is the major obstacle to embodying authentic church life in the world. About three years ago, I came to the conclusions that most institutions we call "churches" are really parachurch organizations, much of the "church work" we do focuses on making something happen on Sunday mornings, and much of the money given goes to pay staff to keep the parachurch functions running.

Here I am at the end of the seventh decade of my life, a child of the church and a professor of theology, having to rethink everything I thought I knew about the place of the church in my life. I invite you to join me in this journey. I welcome especially those disenchanted with institutional churches. Perhaps you are in my generation and feel burned out by years of institutional maintenance and disillusioned with self-perpetuating bureaucracies. Maybe you are thirty-five years of age or younger and have never seen the relevance of institutional churches to your life. Institutional churches appear self-serving, hypocritical, money grubbing, growth obsessed, clergy dominated, and backward. Feel assured that I will not try to convince you that you are wrong. Instead, I want to introduce you to a different vision of church life. It is simple, small, requires no money, needs no clergy, and possesses no property. It does not run like a business, is not organized like a corporation, and does not feel like a theater. It feels like a family, meets around a table, and focuses on the Lord.

1. First Things

I like to get to the bottom of things. I am not satisfied until I see how a claim can be properly derived from a foundation that cannot be further analyzed. I know I am not alone in this desire, but I have been told that I am more obsessed with it than many others. So, as a first step in rethinking church, I want to clarify the essence of the thing we call church.

Essential versus Accidental

When something provokes us to take an interest in a thing and seek greater understanding, our minds begin sorting things, making distinctions, and seeing relationships we had not noticed before. One such distinction turns on the difference between the essential and the accidental features of a thing. Conceptually, there is a clear distinction between the two even if it is difficult to apply in practice. If you add or remove an accidental feature of a car, flower, or human being, they still exist. But if you destroy an essential feature of a thing, it no longer exists. Aristotle said that a human being is essentially a "rational animal." A human being can be short or tall, male or female, or brown or white. But if you remove life or rationality from its concept, it ceases to define a human being. Likewise, distinguishing between the essential and the accidental properties of the church is one way to begin rethinking church.

Adding or subtracting accidental features from a church does not change its essential character. However, removing an essential feature would destroy its churchly existence completely. What is left is no longer the church. Whether a church meets in a public building, a private dwelling, or in a cave, makes no difference to its existence as a church. However, a "church" without faith in Jesus Christ is not a church at all.

We need to exercise great care and humility in applying the essence/accident distinction to the church. Reading church history and observing contemporary churches reveals great diversity in how this distinction has been applied. Many controversies, some of them bitter, find their origin in this diversity. There are at least four types of diversity possible among churches:

1. A church can mistake an accidental feature for an essential one, expanding greatly the number of "essential" features.

2. At the opposite extreme, a church can treat essential features as optional.

3. A church may burden itself with so many and such extraneous accidental features that it becomes almost impossible to live out its essence.

4. A church may be so careful not to add accidental features that it cannot adapt to changing circumstances and carry out its mission effectively.

Options 1, 3, and 4, despite their excesses, deficiencies, and misplaced priorities, preserve the essential features of the church. Only option 2 ceases to be the church at all. Given the possibilities for mistakes and the absence of a perfect alternative, you can see why I want to approach the question of the essence of the church cautiously, methodically, and with humility. Despite the risks, however, to accomplish the goal of this book I must attempt to specify the essential features of the church.

The Church is a Divine Act

Most of us already have an idea of what "church" means—from the Bible, history, and our own experience. However, at this point in the book I am asking everyone to lay all those images aside to join me in rethinking the concept from the foundation up.

To get us started, let me make an assertion: we will find the essence of the church in its origin as documented in the New Testament. Perhaps we can learn more about the full implications of those essential features as the church takes different forms in different cultures and historical eras, but I am working with the assumption that its essence existed from the beginning and has not changed.

The most basic essential feature of the church is its origin in God. In Ephesians 1, we read about the grand story of salvation in Christ, from the depths of eternity (1:4, 11) to the gathering of all things together in Christ (1:10). At first, Paul speaks of the objects of God's great love as "we" and "us" (1:3–10), but soon he begins to include those whom he calls "you" (1:11–18). Toward the end of the chapter, Paul combines the "we" and "you" into a new "us" (1:19) that he calls "God's holy people" (1:18) and "the church, which is his body, the fullness of him who fills everything in every way" (1:22–23).

The church is God's idea, God's choice, and God's act. God created it to achieve his purpose according to his plan. The church is the divine act of gathering all the scattered pieces of creation into unity in Christ by the power of the Spirit (Eph 1:13). We need to think of the word "church," then, not merely as a noun designating an entity but as a verb denoting an action. God is *churching* the shattered and conflicted world. This notion will make better sense if we set aside the English word "church" for a moment and think of the Greek word *ekklesia,* which means a gathering of people, an assembly. A gathering must be gathered by someone for some purpose. God is the one who gathers, and the gathering (the church) is the result of God's act. In rethinking church, then, we must rid ourselves of any view of the church that displaces God as the primary actor and replaces him with human actors. The "gathering" and the "uniting" of all things in Christ that we call "church" is God's work. God is *churching* (reconciling) the world in Christ (2 Cor 5:19).

If we forget this essential feature of the church and try to "make it happen" by our own power, we may achieve great things measured by human standards. We may build huge, wealthy, and influential institutions. We may entice crowds of people to say the right words. But only God can gather the scattered pieces of creation into unity in Christ. Our task is to let ourselves be churched by God. It is to believe, speak, and act only in harmony with the crucified and risen Christ empowered by God's Spirit.

The Body of Christ

Now consider a second essential feature of the church. The church exists in the world only "in Christ" (Rom 8:1, 10; Eph 2:6–7, 10) as "his body" (Eph 1:23; Col 1:24). Christ is the sphere within which the church lives and the form that gives it identity. The church is visible within the world only as his body.

Reconciliation in Christ

Jesus Christ is the place within the world where and when "the Word became flesh and dwelt among us" (John 1:14) and where "God was in Christ reconciling the world to himself" (2 Cor 5:19). In Jesus Christ, God takes one human being through life and death into eternal life through the resurrection. Jesus is both the first truly saved and glorified human being and the Savior of all who follow. Paul speaks of the resurrected Christ as the "last Adam" who has become a "life-giving spirit" (1 Cor. 15:45). Just as in Adam we receive mortal life, in Christ we shall inherit eternal life. As Paul puts it, "For as in Adam all die, so in Christ all will be made alive" (1 Cor 15:22). Or again, "And just as we have borne the image of the earthly man, so shall we bear the image of the heavenly man" (15:49). To be "in Christ" is to be in communion with him, empowered by him, protected by him, directed by him, and transformed by him. By establishing this spiritual space and gathering people into it, Christ establishes and maintains the thing the New Testament calls "church."

The Church Exists as the Body of Christ

The New Testament uses the term "body" in reference to the church in more than one way. In 1 Corinthians 12:12–31, Paul uses the unity and diversity within the human body as a metaphor for the unity and diversity in the church. Ephesians 1:23 and Colossians 1:24 speak of the church as the "body of Christ," which functions in a way similar to how our bodies function, as visible expressions of our persons. Christ manifests himself, speaks, and works visibly, audibly, and palpably in the world through the church. Christ is the head—that is, the governing principle—and life of the body. Apart from the governing principle, the body has no unity or direction. Apart from the life principle, the body has no power to accomplish anything. Any institution where

God is not reconciling the world to himself in Christ is not the church. A group through which Jesus no longer manifests himself in the world is no longer the church. And a "gathering" that no longer understands itself as existing in Christ and drawing its life from him has forgotten its essence.

The Indwelling Spirit

The indwelling of the Holy Spirit is a third essential feature of the church. In the New Testament, especially in Acts and the letters of Paul, the Holy Spirit acts to make God present and effective within the human sphere. The Spirit empowers, leads, purifies, renews, and encourages believers. He gathers, creates, unites, and enlightens the church. He gives life, transforms, liberates, bestows love, and perfects those God has chosen. The Spirit is God's personal presence, elevating human beings above mere human possibility, uniting them with Christ, and making them into God's children. He is the active presence of the future resurrection, the guarantee of the future inheritance. Apart from the Holy Spirit there is no church.

The Divine Dimension

A gathering of people is the "church" only as it is united to God through Christ and the Spirit. Only as it exists in Christ, as the body of Christ, empowered by

God's own Spirit is a "people" the people of God. The church is a divine and a human reality. The divine dimension is not a separable aspect, located in heaven, acting only intermittently. The divine permeates (diffuses) the human aspect and draws the human into the divine life. God's presence and activity in the church is not only essential, it is primary. The church exists because of the divine presence, it acts in divine power, and it moves as directed by divine wisdom. Christ is the head, the Spirit leads, and God is all in all.

Caution Needed

I want to issue a caution at this point. The church possesses a divine dimension as an aspect of its constitution, but this truth should never be used—as it has been too often—by some to bolster their claims to have coercive authority over others. Christ and the Spirit are fully capable of governing and leading God's church, and they do not delegate their divine authority to anyone. Human beings have "authority" only insofar as their lives embody the cross-shaped life of Jesus, and only through their faithful persuasion and obedient wisdom do they have a right to instruct others. A "church" that claims to be a divine institution but does not actually seek God's will and submit to God's authority is not acting as the church.

The Human Dimension

The human dimension is also an essential feature of the church. The church is a gathering of *people.* It is not simply a divine idea or the divine dimension by itself. Divine and human must be united in one community. In the New Testament, the *ekklesia* is called an assembly, a people, a nation (1 Peter 2:9), and a family (Gal 6:10), each denoting human beings in community. The church, then, becomes visible in the world in a community of living human beings.

There are many kinds of assemblies and communities. The church is a people called together by the Spirit of God to live in Christ for the praise and service of God. But the church could not exist apart from a human response to that call. The most basic response is faith. Apart from a believing embrace of the message of Christ, baptism, Eucharist, and other churchly activities make no sense. Faith moves us to turn away from our old lives and mark that transition by receiving baptism, which is pictured in the New Testament as a spiritual washing (Acts 22:16) or a death, burial, and resurrection with Christ (Rom 6:1–7).

The transition from nonbelief to belief and its symbolic enactment in baptism is at once a transition from not being a Christian to being one and from not being a member of the church (or family or people) of God to being included in this people. Becoming a member of the church is not an add-on to becoming a Christian but happens simultaneously and is co-essential. It makes no sense to think one could be "in Christ" but not part of the body of Christ, a child of God but not a member of God's family.

Defining the Church

Until this point in the argument, I have used the term "church" without defining it. For until we uncover the essential features of the church—that is, those factors that determine the difference between its existence and nonexistence—we cannot define it with precision. What, then, is the church? *The church consists of those people who in obedient faith have responded to God's call and by baptism have been incorporated into Christ through the work of the Holy Spirit and, so, have become one body, one people, one family.*

Wherever these factors are present, the church exists in its fullness. Once the church exists and begins to act other factors come into play. Some means will be chosen to organize its life and work. Language and culture, too, will also place their stamp on the outward forms of church life. But it is important not to allow the historical and contemporary forms that the church takes to hide from our sight its simple essence. List any factor you please—clergy, systems of organization, property, employees, legal recognition, social visibility, or tax-exempt status—none are essential. Sweep them all away and the church exists still. The church is simple in essence, hence adaptable in form.

The Christian and the Church

Since New Testament language about the church envisions a community that gathers and acts as one at least on occasion, certain questions about the relationship between the individual Christian and the church arise: (1) Does the church exist in each individual or does the church exist only when formally gathered "as the assembly"? (2) If you were the only Christian alive, would the church still exist? (3) Assuming that the church exists even when not gathered, must an individual Christian gather regularly with other Christians as the church?

The answers to these three questions are implicit in the definition of the church: (1) Yes, the church exists in each individual believer. Each believer is called by God, lives in Christ, and participates in the life of the Spirit. The divine and human dimensions are united even in an individual Christian. The church does not cease to exist when not assembled as a group to act corporately. Christ and the Spirit are not divided by distance. (2) Yes. The church would exist if you were the only Christian in the world. (3) Yes. Though individual Christians can act as members of God's special people even when alone—in prayer, praise, study, witness, and service—the love of God poured into their hearts by the Spirit (Rom 5:5) will drive them into fellowship with others who share that same love. This gathering is a sign of the future unity of all things in Christ "when the times reach their fulfillment" (Eph 1:10).

Questions for Discussion

1. Have you or has someone you know experienced the problems of burnout and disillusionment as they are described in the Preface? How widespread is this problem?

2. Discuss the four ways essential and accidental elements can be related in churches. If you think there are more or less than four types, explain what additions or subtractions you would make to the list.

3. What are some ways in your experience that the church has forgotten that it is God's act? How can we keep this truth in mind and follow it in practice?

4. Discuss the implications of the New Testament teaching that the church is the body of Christ?

5. Discuss the definition of the church given in this chapter. Is anything missing?

2. The Essential Mission

Witness

What is the essential work of the church, the activity that must not be neglected at all costs? The New Testament church did many things. It worshiped, sang, prayed, baptized, participated in the Eucharist, gathered, taught, preached, counseled, and served. But I believe the New Testament vision of the essential work can be captured in one word: *witness*. Peter puts it this way: "You are a chosen people, a royal priesthood, a holy nation, God's special possession, that you may *declare* the praises of him who called you out of darkness into his wonderful light" (1 Peter 2:9). And Paul explains that God's "intent was that now, through the church, the manifold wisdom of God should be *made known* to the rulers and authorities in the heavenly realms, according to his eternal purpose that he accomplished in Christ Jesus our Lord" (Eph 3:10–11).

I am using the verb "to witness" in the broad sense of "to manifest." The church works to manifest on earth what is going on in heaven and to embody in the present the future kingdom of God. The church teaches, proclaims, worships, and lives to make known the character and will of God. It must not let the world go into the night with an easy conscience or a despairing heart. Even if it must speak as a lone voice calling to a "disobedient and obstinate" people (Isa 65:2), even if no one listens, and even if it finds itself persecuted, the church never ceases to call the world to the knowledge of God.

Bearing witness to the goodness and greatness of God demonstrated in Jesus Christ is the essential work of the church. In all it does it must never forsake this task. In its works of mercy and justice, in its worship, teaching, and preaching, in its work with children, teens, young adults, families, and seniors, and in its use of funds and property, its work of witness must never be neglected.

Ecclesiastical Malpractice

While the essential nature and work of the church are fresh on our minds I want to entertain the sad possibility that the church may dilute or abandon its essential work.

The Way of the World

Human beings are social animals. We are born into families and form extra-familial associations of all kinds, from friendships to states. Nature places us in families. Friendships are forged by mutual interests. People create associations to serve a purpose, to achieve an end. Some goals can better be accomplished by the cooperation of many individuals. A thousand people together can achieve what 1,000 individuals working separately cannot.

I cannot speak with authority here, but it seems to me that people usually form associations to deal with a single challenge. Athletic clubs promote their sport. Guilds pursue the economic interests of their professions. Founders establish schools to facilitate education. Learned societies advance their subjects. But it is well known that associations tend to stray from their founding purposes. Energy, influence, and money originally directed to one purpose are diverted to another. This change can happen in several ways. (1) The original founders focused single-mindedly on the end they wished to serve and devoted themselves wholeheartedly to that cause. However, second and third generation leaders often do not share that original vision and devotion. They become bureaucrats devoted to perpetuating the institutional structures of the association. Their work becomes a job rather than a mission. (2) Every association must have officers that discharge responsibilities on behalf of the association. These officers are tempted to place their own interests above the original mission, diverting energy away from the founding goal of the association.

(3) Associations possess power and influence. Their members bestow this power on them so that they can achieve the end for which they were created. But an association's officers are greatly tempted to redirect that power and influence toward ends unrelated to the origi-

nal purpose of the institution. And often those unrelated ends are political. This abuse is the most insidious of the ways associations can be hijacked. It is common, even expected, that associations supposedly devoted to education, a sport, a profession, or a particular subject will make resolutions and public proclamations on divisive political and social issues completely unrelated to their reason for existence. Not all mutinies *(riots)* occur on ships. Not all pirates sail the seas.

The Visible Church

The church exists not only in heaven but on earth. It lives "in Christ," but appears in space and time. It is the body of Christ, but it looks like a collection of human bodies. When the church becomes visible in the world it takes form as a human association. To the world's eyes that is all it is. In analogy to other associations, the church coordinates the resources of its members to achieve its objectives. It must have some organizational structure. And here is the great challenge: the church has always been tempted to follow the path of other associations. (1) Later generations may not feel the passion for the mission that the founding generation felt. They may begin to preserve the traditions of earlier days simply to safeguard their positions in a bureaucracy. (2) Leaders may begin to enjoy the power, honor, and money that their positions bring rather than viewing themselves as means to the end of witness to the glory and goodness of God.

(3) Church leaders may begin to view the church as a means to social and political ends. The church assimilates to the model of service organizations, non-profit groups, or even political lobbies. Like educational, professional, and learned society leaders, the church's leaders may wish to leverage the influence of the church to weigh in on the political and social issues of the day to the detriment of its mission of witness to Jesus Christ.

Essential Practices

My goal in the first part of this book has been to place before our minds the essential features of the New Testament church so that we can use this vision to assess the forms and activities of the contemporary church. Only one more question remains in the first part. Does the New Testament mandate any essential practices that the church must perform?

The issue of church practices moves us into new territory and raises a significant problem. Defining the essential nature of the church as the faithful in Christ and the essential nature of the church's work as witness helps distinguish the universal aspects of the church from first-century culture. Religious practices and their symbolic meanings are always deeply rooted in specific cultures. Had the first-century church designated dozens of its culture-bound practices as essential, it would have been impossible for Christianity to become an enduring, world-wide movement. The first great challenge to the church's universal nature came as the question of which Jewish practices must be incorporated into its life: circumcision, kosher rules, or Sabbath laws? After a long and intense struggle, the view of Paul prevailed: Christians do not have to practice the Jewish law. Faith in Christ is enough. We can only imagine what would have happened had Paul lost this argument.

Baptism

There are two practices, however, that the first-century church passed on as essential: baptism and the Lord's Supper or Eucharist. Like all practices, they have deep cultural roots. Baptism harkens back to the Old Testament's ritual washings, which were continued and modified in Second Temple Judaism (515 BC—70 AD) and in Jewish sects like that at Qumran, in which the faithful were baptized several times a day. These Jewish baptisms enacted ritual, symbolic cleansings to remove defilement and render the object or person qualified for interacting with God. John the Baptist, drawing on these traditions, demanded that Jews of his day repent of their sins and have themselves baptized in preparation for the impending divine judgment on the nation.

Jesus instructed his followers to be baptized and to baptize others. Even though baptism has deep roots in the Old Testament and first-century Judaism, the church has held the practice essential for its life because Jesus instituted it as a permanent practice for his people. The meaning of baptism must be explained with reference to its historical background. Yet, baptism is not completely alien to any culture, for it involves the symbolic use of water as a cleansing and life-giving agent, something universal in all cultures.

The Lord's Supper

The second essential practice is the Lord's Supper in which the church gathers to share a meal in the presence of the Lord. The Supper has deep roots in Jewish identity, deriving from the Passover meal eaten in haste as the Lord delivered his people from Egyptian slavery (Ex 12). The Eucharist must not be uprooted from its background in the Old Testament, for then we will not be able to understand Jesus's adaptation of it to signify his sacrificial act of delivering his people from sin, death, and the devil and creating a new covenant. Like baptism, the Lord's Supper is not alien to any culture, for everyone has to eat and knows the life-giving properties of food. Eating is a social act in every culture.

Notice the simplicity and universal adaptability of the church. The church consists of those who believe and are baptized into Christ, whose work is witness to Christ, and who by participating in the Lord's Supper remember and proclaim Jesus's redemptive sacrifice. The church travels light as it moves from one culture to another and one century to another. It does not center on a holy site, for the Holy Spirit dwells in their bodies and in their midst. It speaks in the common tongue and not in a holy language accessible only to the learned. To make its sacrifices it needs no altars, animals, or priests.

Its whole life is worship and its prayers are its sacrifices. It needs no golden candelabra or silk robes. Its riches are good deeds and its treasures are in heaven. It can be dispossessed of all its worldly goods and lose nothing of substance. It needs no alliances and seeks no privileges from nations and empires. Its citizenship is in heaven, and it pledges allegiance only to the King of kings. It can meet in a basilica, in a private dwelling, by a river, on a street corner, or in a prison cell. It matters not, for the whole world is the temple of the Lord.

Questions for Discussion

1. Explain why you agree or disagree with the assertion that the essential work of the church is witness, understood as manifesting Jesus Christ in word and deed.

2. List and discuss some ways churches and their leaders engage in practices that replace or distort the church's essential mission of witness.

3. Discuss the relationship of the church's two essential practices—baptism and the Lord's Supper—to the essential work of witness.

4. Discuss the nature and practical implications of the church's adaptability to all ages and cultures.

3. The Lure and Threat of Political Power

Is Church Reform Possible?

Now we begin a new phase of our project *Rethinking Church*. I have set out the essential features of the church in three areas: its constitution, work, and practices. Reading church history and observing the church of today make clear that the church never appears in the world in its essential features only. It always embodies itself in forms and uses means derived from human culture. These forms and means are not essential but accidental features. Ideally, in every situation the church would choose forms and means that embody its essence and advance its mission effectively, while never obscuring, hindering, or replacing them.

But in this world conditions are never ideal. Christ and the Spirit are infallible, but we are not. God is holy and sinless, but we need grace and forgiveness. The church looks forward to its future redemption, perfection, and glorification. But it is not there yet. The people of God are sinners, each and all. Its leaders are sinful and fallible. This has been so from the very beginning. Peter and Paul argued vigorously about the nature of the gospel (Gal 2). The Corinthian church suffered divisions (1 Cor. 1–3). Jesus promised that the "gates of Hades will not overcome" the church (Matt 16:18). He did not promise to protect it from all mistakes, sin, and foolishness. Believers are "led by the Spirit" (Rom 8:14), but we must still "live by faith and not by sight" (2 Cor 5:7).

God directs the church to its appointed end despite its sins and errors. He uses fallible leaders and sinful people to work his will. Consequently, from a human point of view the history of the church moves in a zigzag pattern with a lurch to the right followed by a lurch to the left. It takes one step forward and two steps backward. Its path is littered with heresies and schisms, spectacular successes and abysmal failures. It has produced martyrs *and* persecutors, self-denying monks *and* indulgent bishops, peacemakers *and* warriors. But it still exists! Christ is still preached, and sometimes the light pierces the darkness. For a moment we see clearly what is, what could be, and what will be.

What, then, can fallible and sinful people do to reform the church for today? Is it possible to do a better job today of embodying the essential features of the church in the world than we have in the past? With God, all things are possible. But we must not mistake God's possibilities for our abilities. Only with "fear and trembling" (Phil 2:12), humility, grace, self-criticism, diligence, patience, thoughtfulness, penitence, and prayer do we have hope of actually doing more good than harm for the church in our age.

Know Your Enemy

Jesus entered the world to fight a battle. In his baptism, he declared war, not against Rome, the corrupt Jerusalem aristocracy, or the fanatical Zealots, but against the devil and his allies. The devil struck the first blow. "If you are the Son of God," the tempter whispered, "tell these stones to become bread." Jesus replied, "It is written: 'Man shall not live on bread alone, but on every word that comes from the mouth of God'" (Matt 4:3–4). Two more blows followed. All three of the devil's suggestions urged Jesus to adopt the world's understanding of glory, honor, and power. Jesus knows that Rome and Jerusalem are not the real oppressors of God's people. The real enemy is not flesh and blood. The walls of his stronghold cannot be breached with siege works. Nor can he be subdued with arrow and sword. The devil's weapons are half-truths and lies through which he enflames lust for glory, honor, and power and instils fear of humiliation, obscurity, and death. Jesus spoke the truth: God alone deserves our trust.

Jesus rejected worldly glory, honor, and power and accepted death as the price of faithfulness to his Father. But God raised him from the dead! Though in the resurrection the devil's defeat became obvious, the devil had already lost. For the decisive battle did not turn on Jesus's power to resist Rome's decision to crucify him but on his resolve to trust God whatever the cost. Can Jesus remain loyal to God despite every evil the devil can inspire human beings to inflict? The devil's most powerful weapon is the threat of death (Heb 2:14). But Jesus disarmed him of this tool: "Do not be afraid of those who kill the body and after that can do no more" (Luke 12:4). Jesus's faithfulness unto death inflicted a spectacular defeat on the devil! The cross, as Paul proclaims, is God's secret wisdom:

> We do, however, speak a message of wisdom among the mature, but not the wisdom of this age or of the rulers of this age, who are coming to nothing. No, we declare God's wisdom, a mystery that has been hidden and that God destined for our glory before time began. None of the rulers of this age understood it, for if they had, they would not have crucified the Lord of glory. (1 Cor 2:6–8)

Indeed, they would not have! For Jesus's willing acceptance of shame, pain, and death on a Roman cross, instigated by the rulers of this age, demonstrated their slavery to the devil and blindness to the truth. They found themselves powerless to intimidate Jesus's followers into submission. The cross redefined what glory, honor, and power mean for God and human beings. To seek them now means something very different from what it did before the cross. And the rulers of our age understand it no better than the rulers who crucified the Lord of glory.

Do Not Love the World

As the church becomes visible in the world, occupying space and time, turning people toward Christ in devotion and loyalty, and transforming the way people live and relate to others, the world fights back on all fronts. The New Testament uses the word "world" in two distinct ways. It can mean God's creation, which he loves and wishes to save (John 3:16). Or, it can refer to the twisted order that exists in the human mind wherein something other than God holds the place of honor. This perverted order manifests itself in such individual vices as lust, greed, pride, and in all levels and combinations of the social order:

> Do not love the world or anything in the world. If anyone loves the world, love for the Father is not in them. For everything in the world—the lust of the flesh, the lust of the eyes, and the pride of life—comes not from the Father but from the world. The world and its desires pass away, but whoever does the will of God lives forever. (1 John 2:15–17)

Social Conformity

I will leave to one side the individual and focus on the social dimension. We are born into a network of social relationships of ever-increasing abstraction—the biological family, local communities, and finally the state. We join such voluntary associations as businesses, friendships, schools, gangs, clubs, unions, and professional organizations. Each of these societies possesses an identity before we enter it. In volunteer societies, this identity expresses itself in rules and ceremonies, and in the state it is expressed in laws and symbols. Every association demands that its members conform in ways that preserve its identity and help achieve its purpose. Individuals who refuse to conform are disciplined.

According to the New Testament, we should not be surprised but expect the entire social network into which we are born to be wrongly ordered. Everything is out of place. As I said above, the world and everything in it is God's creation. But if we love it more than we love God, we become "the world" in the second sense. Nor can we evade our responsibility by forming associations. Human associations do not escape but mirror and magnify the vices and virtues of the human heart. Sadly, most people do not love the Father more than they love the world. Consequently, the human institutions they form always aim at pleasure, wealth, honor, or security as their chief goals. So much so that John can say, "The whole world is under the control of the evil one" (1 John 5:19).

The State

The state more than any other human institution mirrors and magnifies human vices and virtues. Like other human institutions composed of lovers of the world and dedicated to worldly ends, states cannot love the Father more than they love themselves. More than that, because states by their very nature reserve to themselves the ultimate power of life and death over their individual members, they inevitably come to think of themselves as divine. Perhaps some states are better than others when measured by the gospel. I do not deny this. But whether promulgated *(promoted)* as the will of the Pharaoh of Egypt, the King of Babylon, the Emperor of Rome, or the will of the people speaking through their representatives, the "law" that must be obeyed on pain of death is always a human law. The confession "Jesus is Lord" is heresy in every municipality, county, state, and country in this world in any age. Idolatry is the unofficial religion of every state.

When the church becomes visible in the world, the world expects it to submit. Everyone else does. But the church replies to every family, friendship, business, school, gang, club, union, professional organization, and state, "Jesus is Lord." The church can make this confession in the face of the world's threats only if it remembers Jesus's words: "Do not be afraid of those who kill the body and after that can do no more" (Luke 12:4).

Privilege Comes with a Price

The Persecuted Church

For the first 275 years of its existence, the church endured persecution, spontaneous at the local level, official at the imperial level. Its offense? Non-conformity "to the pattern of this world" (Rom 12:2). Christians would not participate in local pagan ceremonies and sacrifices that accompanied almost every aspect of social life in the Roman Empire. Nor would they pledge loyalty to Rome by offering sacrifices to Caesar.

The Imperial Church

The Edict of Milan in 313, which proclaimed religious freedom within the Eastern part of the Roman Empire, signaled the beginning of the end of official persecution. Constantine's defeat of his co-emperor Licinius in the 324-battle of Chrysopolis brought it to a complete end. The emperor Constantine I (d. 337) favored Christianity and even participated in the Council of Nicaea (325). Theodosius I (d. 395) took the final step toward establishing Christianity as the state religion of the Roman Empire by outlawing many heresies and ending pagan sacrifices. The tables had turned. Christian emperors favored the church and now persecuted pagans in the same way that pagans had previously persecuted Christians.

Not surprisingly, Christians rejoiced, thanked God for their new freedom and privileges, and hailed Constantine as a saint and a thirteenth apostle. Can we blame them? Who wants to live as a social outcast, have your property confiscated, be thrown in jail, or suffer torture and death for being a Christian? What was the persecuted church to do when the Emperor offered it freedom to worship as it pleases and organize its internal affairs as it thinks best? When given official status, financial support, and social visibility, should the church have turned them down? Seeing crowds of people enter the churches for worship and instruction, should the church have turned them away? Most of us would have made the same decisions had we been in their shoes.

The Free Church

Privilege always comes with a price. *For when the empire becomes Christian, the church becomes imperial.* Perhaps most of my readers will agree with me that this exchange turned out to be a Faustian bargain. But I want to argue that getting out of that deal with the devil is not as easy as renouncing established churches and ratifying the First Amendment to the Constitution of the United States: "Congress shall make no law respecting an establishment of religion, or prohibiting the free exercise thereof." As I pointed out previously, every state reserves to itself the power of life and death over all individuals and associations within its jurisdiction. If it leaves the church alone, if it recognizes its freedom to worship as it pleases, to organize as it sees fit, to choose its own leaders, and if it grants such privileges as tax-exempt status, it does so only because it judges that the church does not work against the essential interests of the state.

A state may view its interests in ways that harmonize with the church's mission of witness. It may consider the work of the church a valuable contribution to the common good. If so, it is not always wrong for the church to use these freedoms and privileges to advance its mission. However, in every society, no matter how friendly to the church, there will always be areas where the state's aims cut across the church's mission. There are no exceptions to this rule, for "no one can serve two masters" (Matt 6:24). In some cases, friendly states' views of their interests can change so dramatically as to come into fundamental conflict with the church. The church always faces the temptation to hold on to its freedoms and privileges by subordinating, compromising, or giving up its mission of witnessing to the lordship of Jesus Christ.

At every point in its relationship to the world, from bare toleration, to approval, to establishment, the church should consider the price it must pay for these freedoms and privileges. How deep in debt we have already become may not become clear until the mortgage comes due. And come due it will. Perhaps it already has.

The Quest for Visibility

A church with any visibility at all will have a relationship to the state—as persecuted, free, free and privileged, or established. Every state claims the right to decide what behaviors and beliefs of individuals and groups within its jurisdiction support or threaten its interests. It reserves exclusive power to dispossess, incarcerate, or kill anyone it deems a threat. Hence, the church must always maintain awareness of this "elephant in the room" even if the elephant seems very friendly at the moment. How, then, should the church relate to such states as the United States and other Western democracies that acknowledge its freedom and grant it certain privileges?

A City on a Hill

Many contemporary believers have never questioned the assumption that the church should seek maximum visibility in society and take full advantage of whatever freedom it has to get its message out. After all, Jesus told his disciples to proclaim the good news to the whole world (Matt 28:18–20; Luke 24:47; Acts 1:8). We are supposed to "let our light shine":

> You are the light of the world. A town built on a hill cannot be hidden. Neither do people light a lamp and put it under a bowl. Instead, they put it on its stand, and it gives light to everyone in the house. In the same way, let your light shine before others, that they may see your good deeds and glorify your Father in heaven. (Matt 5:14–16)

Let Your Light Shine

I understand the desire for visibility, and I can see why people take Jesus's statements as grounds for seeking it. But we need to ask what Jesus meant by "let your light shine." I am certain that Jesus did not intend to mandate building cathedrals and huge church buildings, wearing crosses and clerical dress, or getting a Christian tattoo

35

and putting a fish bumper sticker on your car. Of course, Jesus did not forbid them either, and they can witness to the faith. They can also symbolize social power and wealth. Building an expensive church building is similar in some ways to planting a flag. It says, "We are here and are a force to be reckoned with." Such visibility can be more intimidating than inviting to outsiders. Or, it can obscure the gospel by associating it with material advantages. I can understand wanting to be part of something big, powerful, and wealthy. It is a natural human desire. But I think Jesus had something else in mind.

It seems more likely, given its context in the Sermon on the Mount (Matt 5–7), that "let your light shine" means taking seriously our responsibility to live every day and in every relationship in vivid awareness of the love of God flowing through us to others. Let constant awareness of your Father in heaven impart to you heightened sensitivity to the needs of others. The good you do will bring glory to the Father because it will be evident that your good works are inspired by the Father. The "light" Jesus speaks of is not that of a spotlight illuminating a 100-foot cross on a hill above Interstate 405. It is not the light reflected off cathedrals, church buildings, and gold cross pendants. It is the lives of people that speak and act in witness to the love of God revealed in the face of Jesus. Nothing else is required.

Coming to see that the church can exercise fully its responsibility of witness without great social visibility can free us from the inordinate urge to seek it and from incautious use of religious freedom granted by the "friendly elephant." For what the state gives, it can take away.

The Ambiguity of Privilege

In 1833, Massachusetts became the last state to end its system of state support for churches. Since that time churches in the United States have been officially free and privileged but not established. In the previous paragraphs, I focused on religious freedom and its dangers. Now I want to examine the idea of privilege and its temptations.

What is Privilege?

The word privilege has a long history and many meanings. According to the *Oxford Dictionary of the English Language,* it derives ultimately from Latin in the days of Cicero (106 – 43 BC). *Privilegium* combines two Latin words, one meaning "private" and the other "law." The word was first used in a negative sense, as a law disadvantaging an individual or group. Later it acquired the positive sense in which we use the English word today. In this core sense, a privilege is an exception given to an individual or group to a law binding on others or a positive benefit bestowed by law on some but not everyone. Even though today we use it of special advantages some people have over others no matter how they were acquired—by birth or good fortune or successful labor or in execution of an official duty—it still possesses an aura of unfairness that provokes resentment and envy from those not so privileged.

The Church and Privilege

Many privileges enjoyed by the church today are also enjoyed by other nonprofit corporations, specifically those under the IRS classification "Charitable and Religious Organizations" [IRS code 501(c) (3)]. Under these regulations, churches are exempt from paying certain taxes, and a portion of contributions by individuals to those organizations receive favorable tax status. The United States government gives Christian churches and charitable organizations, along with other religious groups, special exceptions in deference to the First Amendment to the Constitution. For example, churches and some religious nonprofits claim exemptions from certain parts of anti-discrimination laws applicable to other groups. Below is a typical statement of non-discrimination written for nonprofit organizations:

> [My Organization] is committed to equal employment and volunteer opportunity without regard to age, ancestry, disability, national or ethnic origin, race, religious belief, sex, sexual orientation, gender identity, marital status, political belief, or veteran status. (Quoted by permission from https://www.brindlefoundation.org/non-discrimination)

Religious nonprofit organizations often place exception clauses within these declarations claiming exemptions based on freedom of religion. Some simply say, "[Organization X] does not *unlawfully* discriminate...." Others add explanations such as the following, "[Organization Y] *is exempt from certain state and federal anti-discrimination laws based on its status as a religious non-profit corporation and its religious beliefs.*"

The Cost of Privilege

The advantages of privilege are obvious and difficult to turn down when offered. As you can see from the discussion above, privileges granted to churches fall into two categories, financial and exemption from anti-discrimination laws. These privileges greatly advance the work of churches in so far as they are organized as legal, corporate entities that engage in commercial activity. I do not think it is an exaggeration to say that revoking these privileges would destroy most churches as they are currently organized. For churches could not continue to do business as usual if they were subjected to taxation on income and property and individual contributions to churches were to become taxable. Were churches to become subject to the full range of anti-discrimination laws they would be forced to hire atheists, heretics, and immoral people as ministers. They could become subject to laws targeting hate speech for teaching biblical morality.

In recent years, churches and other Christian nonprofit organizations in the United States and other Western countries have come under growing pressure to conform to the dominant culture of non-discrimination.

Calls to revoke the church's privileges and exemptions have grown more insistent. As tempting as it is to enter this culture war, I want to look at this issue from another angle. My concern in this book is preserving the church's essential nature as the body of Christ and its essential mission of witness to Jesus, not defending its privileges.

The privileges granted by the state apply only to that dimension of the church that is visible to the state as a corporate entity engaged in commerce. Clearly, only churches that exist as legal entities could be "destroyed" by losing their privileges. Only they can be blackmailed by threats of such revocation. Churches that refrain from organizing in this way do not receive privileges from the state. But they also do not need them or fear losing them. Nor are they in danger of mistaking them for the essence of the church.

I do not want to be misunderstood. I do not believe that churches that organize themselves in ways designed to take advantage of state-granted privileges are necessarily doing wrong. I am certainly not calling on the state to take away the church's privileges. I am simply urging the church to count the cost of accepting state granted privileges and to cease thinking of them as unmixed blessings. For if we believe that losing our privileges would destroy the church, we will be greatly tempted to do whatever it takes to preserve them. I want the church to free itself from this fear. The existence of the church and the vitality of its mission do not depend on favors from the state. Even if the church gave up all its current privileges and ceased to exist as a legal entity, it would not thereby cease to exist in its fullness as the body of Christ. Nor would its witness to Jesus become ineffective. Even if we do not choose this path— and most churches will not and perhaps should not do so—it is liberating to know that it is available.

The Church and the Common Good

Since the Fourth Century, the church has functioned within Western society in the role of a supporting player. It served as a teacher of morals, a pastor of souls, and a guarantor of the worldview that made sense of life. The church accompanied you through all of life's passages with her sacraments: at birth with baptism, passage into adulthood with confirmation, transition into the married state with holy matrimony, and in your journey through death with last rites. Along the way, she helped unburden your conscience through the sacraments of penance and Eucharist. The church was involved in education and ministry to the poor. Feast and fast days, Sundays, saint's days, and holy days of all sorts marked out time and gave rhythm to life.

The sixteenth-century Protestant Reformation did not fundamentally reorder this symbiotic relationship between church and society. Looking back with the benefit of hindsight at the late Seventeenth and Eighteenth Centuries, we can see some early indicators of the coming change. However, it was not until the late Nineteenth and early Twentieth Centuries—after Marx, Darwin, Spencer, Dewey, and Freud—that the exponential growth of cities and rapid industrialization produced the beginnings of secular society in the United States. There had always been a large minority of unchurched people. But even the unchurched thought of themselves as Christians and viewed the institutional church as a social good.

The current institutional form of the church in the United States derives from the Nineteenth Century, the era after the legal separation of church and state and before thorough secularization. Churches of today do not expect to receive financial support from the government, but they still claim to serve the common good and wish to retain all their traditional privileges. Accordingly, they presume the right to speak to the moral, social, and political issues of the day.

However, in the early Twenty-First Century there exists a significant minority in Western society that no longer thinks of the church as a social good. This minority is especially critical of traditional morality, and it no longer views the church as a reliable teacher of morals. Indeed, many view the church as systemically sexist, homophobic, transphobic, and racist. Its critics portray it as a purveyor of hate and a hindrance to social progress.

What is to be Done?

Since I am speaking in this book autobiographically and from experience, I hesitate to generalize. However, I do not think that the status quo can be maintained for much longer. Some secular progressives would like to destroy the church by using government power to tax and regulate it into oblivion. Others hope to cancel its speech with interruption and protest. But I think the greatest threat to the church's Christian character is its own unwillingness to rethink its centuries-old supporting role in society at large. As a whole, society no longer looks to the church as its conscience, teacher, pastor, or guarantor of a meaningful worldview. Consequently, the church stands at a crossroad. On the one hand, the broad road beckons. It can try to prove its continued relevance to society by adapting to society's progressive morality while deceiving itself into thinking that this new morality is thoroughly Christian. In contrast, the church can give up its vain ambition to be recognized as chaplain and advisor to an increasingly pagan culture and take up its original mission as a countercultural witness to Christ crucified and risen from the dead. Perhaps the church would do well to remember what Jesus said about our anxious desire to survive: *"For whoever wants to save their life will lose it, but whoever loses their life for me and for the gospel will save it"* (Mark 8:35). This truth applies to churches as well as to individuals.

Questions for Discussion

1. Discuss the significance of the three temptations Jesus faced at the beginning of his ministry and

their continued relevance as temptations the church faces today.

2. How did Jesus defeat the "rulers of this age" on the cross? See 1 Corinthians 2:6–8 in its context of the first two chapters of 1 Corinthians.

3. In what ways should John's warning, "Do not love the world" (1 John 2:15–17), inform how we negotiate our relationship with secular institutions and associations and with the state? Explain why you agree or disagree with the assertion that "Idolatry is the unofficial religion of every state"?

4. Discuss the different ways the church can relate to the state: persecuted, free, free and privileged, and established. What is the significance of the statement, "When the empire becomes Christian the church becomes imperial"?

5. Discuss the idea of privilege in relation to the church's relationship to society. Do you think "privilege comes with a price"? In what ways is privilege an advantage to the church's goal of witness and in what ways does it hinder it?

6. Discuss Jesus's command to "Let your light shine" in relation to the church's quest for visibility in culture.

7. Why do you agree or disagree with the chapter's warning to churches about accepting the social obligation to "serve the common good"?

4. Must Churches be Complicated, Time Consuming, and Expensive?

Adaptability

When the church comes to exist in a particular place and time, it inevitably takes shape as a visible association of people. We can see this happening before our eyes in the New Testament.

Organization

Jesus chose twelve apostles and gathered many others around him. The number twelve, clearly patterned after the twelve tribes of Israel, represents a new beginning to the people of God. In other ways, Jesus and his disciples resembled a school with Jesus as the rabbi. Early Jewish churches naturally adopted the synagogue model. As we can see in Acts, early Christians met in public spaces to listen to the apostles' teaching and in homes to share the Lord's Supper. As the church moved into the gentile world it borrowed models from Greek and Roman cultures. Many groups met in the homes of wealthy patrons, like those gathering in the houses of

Aquila and Priscilla (1 Cor 16:19) and Nympha (Col 4:15). [For this story, see Wayne Meeks, *The First Urban Christians*].

According to Acts, the first church was led by the apostles. Soon other leaders were appointed to administer some community tasks (Acts 6), and eventually James the Lord's brother and the "elders" became the main leaders (Acts 15, Gal 1–2). In the Old Testament, elders were traditional local, tribal, or clan leaders. The authority of elders is a natural extension of the family, and their presence was common among ancient Israel's neighbors and in Greek and Roman villages. As the name indicates, they were usually older men who were respected by the community. In many cities beyond Judea, missionary founders of churches, such as Paul and Barnabas, were the authority figures at least for a time. Apparently, some churches eventually adopted the model of elders as city-wide leaders (Acts 20:7; 1 Tim 5:17; Titus 1:5; James 5:14; 1 Peter 5:1).

In previous chapters, we found in the New Testament clear teaching about what the church is and what it is supposed to do, but we did not find instructions specifying how it must be organized everywhere and for all time, where to assemble to engage in its communal life, or what methods it should use to accomplish its mission. Instead, we find variety on all three counts. Believers seem to be able to adapt to circumstances, modifying as necessary models already used by other types of associations.

Guidance

It seems that there is no one pattern of organization, communal life, or means of action that is essential to the church. Are we, then, left without guidance for these areas? No, I do not think we are left without guidance. First, there is tradition. The New Testament church developed in continuity with Jesus's ministry. It adapted that original community life to new circumstances without making a radical break. Judging by the way it preserved Jesus's teaching and deeds, the early church seems to have treasured that continuity. And in our efforts to be the church Jesus built we should take pains to preserve that continuity as well.

Second, the New Testament's clear teaching about the church's essential constitution and mission gives guidance and sets limits to how we organize and conduct communal life and carry out the church's mission. It should be obvious that organizational structures, functions, offices, and means should serve the church's essence and mission. But experience teaches that they tend to become institutionalized, centralized, and self-perpetuating. Alternative motives and goals gradually eclipse the original motives and goals. Church history can be written as a tug of war between the tendency to drift away from and efforts to return to the church's essential features. Hence, the church in every age must take care to keep its means aligned with its essence and mission. The rest of this book will be devoted to examining the way we conduct church life in contemporary

America (USA) in view of the church's essence and mission.

Simplicity

I am not writing a church history or a survey of church doctrine and practice. There are many related questions I cannot address if I am to stick to my original plan. I am reassessing my place in churches of the type I have attended all my life, the type my students and friends attend. These churches hold with varying degrees of intensity to evangelical theology and piety *(devotion)*. They are mostly non-denominational, or at least they have a great deal of local control. I believe that many others find themselves in similar situations and are also in the process of reexamining the ways they embody their Christian faith in church life. My hope is that others will benefit from thinking along with me.

Churches and Parachurch Organizations

I have come to believe that most organizations that call themselves churches are really ministries of the church or parachurch organizations. They are inspired by the New Testament vision of the church as the body of Christ and are motivated by its mission of witness to Jesus. They do much good work—ministry to families, children, singles, and seniors. They provide large meeting places where hundreds of believers can meet at the same time to experience worship and teaching. They establish homeless ministries, teach English as a second language, create prison ministries, provide daycare for working parents, and much more. However, in many cases, the church's essential nature, activity, and mission are obscured by concerns that could better be dealt with through parachurch organizations devoted to these matters. By adding these features to their agendas and organizing themselves in the ways required for accomplishing these tasks efficiently, churches transform themselves into parachurch churches or simply parachurches.[1]

Do not get me wrong. I do not object to the existence of parachurches. I believe they have a place. But I object when these institutions claim to be identical to the essential church and imply that to participate fully in the people of God you must join this type of organization and give lots of money and time to it. This is not true. You do not have to join a parachurch to be a good Christian and participate fully in the body of Christ. A church can be everything that the church is supposed to be, do everything it is supposed to do, and work effectively toward fulfilling its mission with a few believers meeting in a home or under a tree. This type of church needs no common treasury, no employees, no property, no government entanglement, and no professional clergy. I do not want to idealize the small house church as purely and simply the essential church, acting only in

---

[1]From now on I will be using the nouns "parachurch" and "parachurches" instead of the awkward expression "parachurch church."

essential ways, and having no goals other than the essential goal of witness. However, I am clear that it is closer to that ideal than the complicated and expensive organizations that we usually call churches.

Many parachurches realize that meeting in large assemblies, though having many advantages, cannot facilitate the intimacy, friendship, and deep community that can be created in regular meetings of small groups. But parachurches tend to view their "small group ministries" as adjuncts to the larger church. My dream is to see this priority reversed. You do not have to be a member of a parachurch to be a faithful Christian, but if you want to do so, think of it as an adjunct to the small church where community in Christ really happens. This reversal would of necessity require parachurches to repurpose themselves as organizations designed to facilitate small churches getting together periodically to encourage each other and cooperate on larger projects. This reversal is unlikely to happen, I understand, but from now on, I plan on treating the parachurches I attend in this way.

Money

Let us talk about money as a corrupting force in the life of the church. Jesus spoke to this problem when he said, "You cannot serve both God and money" (Matt 6:24). And 1 Timothy states in clear terms, "The love of money is the root of all evil" (6:10). Of course, money does not force you to love it. But experience teaches us that it is a very effective persuader! You can make money serve you, but it often turns out the other way around. Money is an abstraction, a means of exchange that enables the acquisition of real goods—food, clothing, shelter, beautiful things, and services. These things can serve human needs and produce joy, but they can also be abused and create misery. By pooling the resources of its members a church can acquire more of these things and use them for greater good. This is the ideal anyway. But ideals are rarely realized completely.

Pass the Collection Plate

Consider the churches I designated "parachurches" in the previous section. They conduct their work in ways that require a constant stream of revenue. They purchase and maintain building complexes, making it necessary to hire janitors, make periodic repairs, and pay large utility bills. To coordinate the activities of hundreds of people and programs for every age and interest group, churches must hire five, ten, or even twenty-five ministers. The Sunday worship alone requires the services of a worship minister, sound and lighting technicians, singers, and several band or orchestra members. Such an operation requires support from a large secretarial and bookkeeping staff. Even a medium-sized church needs an annual budget of $800,000 to $1,000,000. Megachurches need $10,000,000 to $50,000,000 annually.

And from where does this money come? It comes from member donations. And why do they give? I do not know all the reasons, and I speak only from my own experience. I am sure most of them give because they believe that their churches do good things with the money. They feel proud of participating in these large-scale good works, which they could not accomplish by themselves. However, I think additional factors are at work. Some churches teach explicitly and others imply that giving to the church is a Christian duty or even a quasi-sacrament. That is to say, giving is considered a meritorious work or a kind of bloodless sacrifice, a required act of worship distinct from the practical purpose for which the gift is used. Or, we think of our gifts as membership dues. We attend church services, enjoy the pageantry and an uplifting message from a gifted speaker, and benefit from the work of staff and volunteers. We feel guilty if we attend without helping to pay for the services.

But money exerts a corrupting force. Churches have earned a reputation for constantly soliciting donations, a reputation nearly universal among outsiders but also common among loyal members. Churches need to meet their annual budgets. The staff's livelihood and the viability of many programs depend on it. Many churches "pass the collection plate" every Sunday. You either contribute or not in front of everyone around you, especially the "deacons" who are passing the plates. The church seems to be of two minds on money versus people. Everyone is welcome, poor as well as rich. "Come as you are," as a popular hymn invites. But do they really mean it, or will it be a "bait and switch" operation? Do churches want to grow because they want everyone to know Jesus and the joy of faith, hope, and love? Or, do they wish to keep the income stream flowing? Because churches have organized themselves in ways that require large numbers of volunteers and lots of money, the good news of the love of Jesus and the free gift of God gets mixed with a less noble message.

Ministers and Money

I want to speak next from personal experience. As a younger person, I served as a paid minister for eight years. I entered the ministry because of a divine call to which I could not say no. I responded in obedience to God. But when I became an employee of a church my duty to God got confused with the expectations of my employer. I could no longer be sure of my motives. I learned a bitter lesson. If your service to God becomes a means of livelihood on which your family depends for mortgage payments, childcare, health insurance, car payments, school loan payments, and retirement savings, the joy of ministry often departs. You begin to think about salary, benefits, and working conditions. You notice who has power over you and who does not. Later in life, I served as an elder in a church where part of my duty was supervising the ministry staff. In that role, my partnership with the ministers in the work of the Lord was made joyless by the need to deal with their concerns having to do with salary, benefits, and working conditions. Money is indeed the root of all evil!

If you have been following my argument so far, you know that I favor small group churches over para-churches. We could go a long way toward removing the corrosive effect of money if churches met in homes, took no collections, made no budgets, owned no common property, and had no employees. I do not think I am naïve about this. There would still be occasions for greed and envy, shame and pride, because of differences among individual believers. But at least the church would not be always seeking donations to run its operations. It would operate more like a family than a business.

The Clergy System

It is time to rethink the idea of the church as an employer of ministers. We will examine this issue from the perspectives of the spiritual life of the minister and of the church as an employer of ministers. We will consider the spiritual advantages and disadvantages of the paid ministry.

This is Personal

As I said in the previous section, this issue is personal for me. I received a divine call into ministry as a college student. Based on that call I changed my major from Chemistry to Bible. To prepare myself for a life of church leadership I spent four years in graduate school working on a Master of Theology degree. Many friends in my own generation entered the ministry and served for many years. Many of my heroes are great preachers and missionaries. And now that I have been teaching theology for thirty-one years in a university that grants two graduate degrees designed to prepare people for fulltime ministry, I have scores of former students in fulltime church ministry.

I share this background because I want you to know that I do not doubt the divine origin of my call into the ministry. Nor do I wish to make any negative judgment about the fine men and women who serve in churches all over the world. Quite the opposite, I want to encourage them in their work and support them in whatever ways I am able.

The Divine Call

Throughout the history of the people of God in the Old and New Testaments and the history of the church from the First to the Twenty-First Century, some men and women have felt compelled by a divine call to speak, preach, teach, and serve in the name of the Lord. Such prophets as Elijah, Amos, Isaiah, Jeremiah, and Ezekiel and the priests deriving from the family of Aaron and the Levites were called into special divine service. Some of these people lived from tithe offerings given by the people and some supported themselves. Jesus called twelve apostles for the special ministry of preaching the gospel to Jews and consolidating the fledgling church. Paul received a call from the resurrected Jesus to preach to the gentiles. In some cases, the apostles and other Christian missionaries, teachers, prophets, and elders received economic help from other believers (1 Cor 9:3–18).

The church needs these services and functions, and Christ himself calls people into these ministries (Eph. 4:11–12). But not everyone is gifted and called to the same role. Paul devoted a whole chapter of 1 Corinthians to this subject. I will quote just three verses: "Just as a body, though one, has many parts, but all its many parts form one body, so it is with Christ. For we were all baptized by one Spirit so as to form one body—whether Jews or Gentiles, slave or free—and we were all given the one Spirit to drink. Even so, the body is not made up of one part but of many" (12:12–14). Some people find themselves gifted and called to teach, preach, and minister in leadership. They devote themselves to study, prayer, and practice to prepare themselves for service. And we are right to thank God for his gift of these people to the church.

But we must distinguish between God's gifting and calling of men and women into his service and taking a job with a church as a paid minister. The two *may* go together, but they are not bound to do so. Hence, my admiration and praise for people gifted and called into ministry does not necessarily translate into admiration and praise for the clergy system as it now stands. You can accept that divine call to evangelize, teach, and preach without becoming clergy. And simply because you earn a degree in ministry and convince a church to hire you does not guarantee that you are doing the work of the Lord.

Interesting

Advantages of the Professional Ministry

The advantages of parachurches hiring people to organize and lead ministries are obvious. (1) It would be nearly impossible for large churches to function as they currently do with an all-volunteer staff. People are busy, and most do not have the training they need to perform some of these functions. Some tasks require many hours a week to carry out. (2) Modern urban and suburban professionals demand highly educated, professional, and skilled people to lead their churches. After all, the corporations for which they work demand such professionalism. (3) Relieving gifted and called men and women of the necessity of spending most of their time working in "secular" work, frees more time for doing the work of ministry. (4) The fourth advantage assumes that the modern church needs ministers with a high level of theological education. Without the prospect of a paid ministry position, young people might not be willing to devote seven years of their lives to acquire the college and seminary training needed for ministry in the modern world. In that amount of time they could train for a high paying secular career.

Notice that advantages (1), (2), and (4) presuppose the existence of big parachurches operating in the ways such churches have for the last hundred years. Of course, these churches need highly educated, skilled, professional ministers. But if you call into question the exclusive legitimacy of the big church model, these advantages become less decisive. If you gather around a table to share a meal, read the Scriptures, and pray for each other, you do not need a highly skilled speaker, a talented worship leader, an efficient administrator, or a meticulous bookkeeper.

Problems with the Clergy System

Now I want to consider some problems that beset the clergy system.

The Spiritual Life of the Clergy

I believe that most people who enter the professional ministry do so because they feel a divine call and want to serve the people of God. They have a warm personal faith and want to serve the Lord freely and happily. However, becoming an employee of a church introduces a new dimension. You now become responsible to a church and its leaders and are no longer free to speak, write, and serve as you please. Your time is not your own, and your family life is everybody's business. Of course, every job comes with restrictions and responsibilities, but this job entangles itself with your relationship with God. Even if your church employer never asks you to do anything that violates your conscience, how do you know whether, without being aware of it, you are trying to please the church when you should be endeavoring to please the Lord? And most insidiously, after a few years ministers are tempted to think of their ministries as they would other jobs, as means of livelihood. If paid ministers are not careful, the work they began freely and joyously in response to a divine call will become a heavy burden. Spiritually exhausted and embittered, they look for a way out.

The Clergy/Laity Divide

The ideas of the ordained clergy and the paid ministry are not identical, although they often overlap. The New Testament makes a distinction among various functions within the church, and some possess a kind of authority. Jesus chose twelve apostles for a special ministry. Their central claim to spiritual authority was their unique relationship to Jesus. They witnessed his teaching, miracles, and death with their own eyes and ears. They also witnessed the empty tomb and encountered the risen Jesus. The core of their unique authority, then, was their first-hand knowledge of Jesus. Paul came later and rested his authority on having been chosen and called by the risen Jesus.

Apostolic witness and authority functions today only through the apostolic teaching, which is contained in the New Testament. No human being living today possesses spiritual authority to speak in God's name or make judgments about another person's relationship to God except as they are faithful to the original apostolic teaching. No person owes spiritual obedience to another human being except as they trust that their counsel articulates the apostolic teaching. In my view, the spiritual authority of a person accrues today not by a ceremony called "ordination" conducted by an authoritative church body but by a life that demonstrates deep knowledge, faithfulness, sincere love, wisdom, and holiness. In short, no one claiming "clergy" status possesses spiritual authority within the church to demand obedience from "lay" believers. Only if their lives demonstrate those qualities mentioned above do they have spiritual authority. Even that authority is the persuasive power of their words and lives.

Why do I insist on breaching the wall between clergy and laity? Clergy often give airs of having special access to God and use this status to maintain power and privilege for selfish reasons. Sometimes the "laity" are quite content to let clergy play this game because it gives them an excuse for their spiritual laziness. Clearly some division of labor is required within the church. But every believer is called to the virtues of faith, hope, and love. The Spirit works to transform everyone into the image of Christ. And all Christians have a responsibility to use their lives in service to the Lord. We are all in our own way preachers, evangelists, missionaries, pastors, and counselors. Everyone is a theologian, because none of us may allow others to think for us. No one is allowed to hand their conscience over to another human being!

Clergy Self-Interest and the Mission of the Church

As I pointed out early in the book, the essential mission of the church is witness to Jesus Christ in life, word, and deed. The work of the church is helping people come to deep faith and be transformed into the image of Christ. One of the greatest temptations of paid ministers is to view the mission and work of the church through the lens of their own self-interest. Clearly, the church can do its work and pursue its mission without seeking to become large, wealthy, famous, and powerful. However, the self-interest of the clergy often aligns with such ambitions. Indeed, it seems that the parachurch model and the clergy system are fraternal twins.

When faced with decisions about the direction the church should take, can clergy seriously consider options that would embody the nature and mission of the church but go against their private interests? Even if as individual believers they wish to pursue only the essential work and mission of the church, the swift current of the clergy system sweeps them downstream, no matter how hard they swim for the shore. Given the dangers of combining the parachurch model and the clergy system, we can justify paraphrasing Jesus's words about the rich in this way: How hard it is for the clergy to enter the kingdom! It is easier for a camel to go through the eye of a needle than for a senior pastor to enter the kingdom of heaven. With human beings this is impossible but with God, all things are possible! (cf. Matt 19:23–26).

Questions for Discussion

1. Explain why you agree or disagree with the chapter's argument that whereas the church's essential nature and mission cannot be changed, it has great flexibility in the ways it organizes itself.

2. Explain why you agree or disagree with the chapter's assertion that most traditional churches should be considered parachurch organizations. Discuss the contention that the usual relationship between small groups and traditional churches should be reversed, that is, with parachurches conceived as ancillary to small group churches.

3. Discuss the issue of churches and money. Do you think churches have become too dependent on things money can buy?

4. Consider the issues of professional ministers and money. What do you think of my experience in this area?

5. Explore the implications of the distinction between those called into God's service and the professional ministry?

6. Discuss the four advantages of the professional ministry. Feel free to list and discuss other advantages.

7. Discuss the two problems with the professional clergy role detailed by the chapter, that is, (1) the challenge to the spiritual life of the minister and (2) the false distinction between clergy and laity.

8. Explore the possibility that the private self-interest of the clergy may conflict with the course of action demanded by the essence and mission of the church. Give examples.

5. The Sunday Gathering: Worship, Instruction, and Fellowship

We move now from considering the organizational structures, finances, and clergy systems that characterize most contemporary churches and shift our attention to the Sunday gathering. What goes on at a typical Sunday gathering of an evangelical, Bible, or community church? And why do such churches gather? I think we can place the Sunday activities of these churches into three general categories: worship, instruction, and fellowship. Ideally, these three types of activity aim at forming the church as a group and as individuals into the image of Christ.

Two Models of Worship

From the Heart

It would be worth our time to examine all biblical words and activities related to worship, but I can achieve my limited purpose by working from a general idea of worship. *Worship is a God-directed activity that attempts in thought, word, bodily position and movement, or symbolic use of elements of creation to express a fitting response to the being, character, and action of God.* In worship, we place before our minds the greatness, goodness, beauty, generosity, and love of God. God demonstrates these qualities in the wonders of creation, in acts of salvation and judgment experienced and told by the prophets and poets of ancient Israel, and most of all in the life, words, miracles, death, and resurrection of Jesus Christ. In worship, we express awe at God's greatness, gratitude for his generosity, praise for his excellence, longing for his presence, and amazement at his love.

Strictly speaking, worship is an individual act. It must come from the heart and express the true thoughts and affections of the individual worshiper. Certainly, the presence of others of like faith enhances our worship. We find others' expressions of worship resonating with our own and increasing our sense of God's presence and glory. Hearing others sing, pray, praise, witness, and explain the scriptures can enhance our perception of God's presence, praiseworthiness, greatness, and love. Some are gifted to articulate in words what others can only feel. Many eyes and ears can perceive and many voices can express what one cannot. Hence, corporate worship can be transformative. The transforming power does not derive from the number of people praising God but from the vision of God that together we see. And for worship to be authentic and transformative, each person must see with their own eyes, hear with their own ears, and express their own hearts.

Communal Worship

I understand the desire to attend worship at a large gathering in a state-of-the-art facility and to be led in worship by talented professionals. The music is excellent, the lighting perfect, and the stage presence of the worship leaders impressive. The worship flows smoothly. Sound fills the hall. Just witnessing a sea of people standing to sing and raising their hands gives one a feeling of confidence and spiritual power. But as someone who served as a church leader in one role or another for forty years, I ask myself about the cost in financial resources and volunteer time to make this event happen. Is it worth it? More importantly, does this impressive event accomplish the purpose of corporate worship better than less elaborate and costly gatherings? If we gather to encounter God's greatness and love and express our wonder and gratitude with the goal of transformation into the image of Christ, I do not see any decisive advantage. Twenty believers gathered in a living room can accomplish the same objective. No doubt a large gathering, because of its greater resources, can do things a small group cannot. But the reverse is also true. In an assembly of 2,000 people, 1,950 will be completely unknown to us. For most of the time, we sit in rows looking at what is happening on stage. Senior pastors are like the celebrities we see on the screen. We feel like we know them, but we have never had a meal with them. In a small gathering we can hear from everyone, we can learn their stories, see their faces, and hear their voices. There is no stage, no spotlight, and no microphone. We know their names and the names of their parents and children. We know their concerns. We grow to love them in the concreteness of their everyday lives, and we are available to each other throughout the week. Worshiping with this church is really transforming.

Of course, these two models are not mutually exclusive. We can choose one or the other or combine them. Whatever the choice, we should measure what we actually do as churches against the essential nature and goal of the church.

The Sermon

The Sermon as Instruction

Christianity's understanding of God and our duties to God are communicated in a story that must be told and told again. No one is born knowing the religious stories, traditions, and myths of their people. This is true even of religions based on the cycles and powers of nature. It is even truer of Christianity, which incorporates the story of Israel—of Abraham, Moses, David, and the prophets—into the New Testament story of Jesus and the teaching of the apostles. New converts and children must be taught this big story and how to live within it. No one is released from the school of Christ except by death.

Instruction is all the more important in situations where Christians are a minority and the surrounding culture is pagan and hostile. The pagan story is told in the daily activities of commerce, law, entertainment, and education. If faith is to survive we must intentionally retreat to places where the Christian story is repeated and lived. The Christian household and the church gathering are the two most important places where this takes place. In these two settings we are often encouraged to develop a routine of individual Bible reading and study.

I have always had a romantic view of preaching. As a college student, I took courses in preaching and as a graduate student, I loved my course on the history of preaching. Preaching and the sermon have always had a place in the life of the church. Jesus taught in the fields and in the synagogues. The apostles and early missionaries preached the gospel to Jews and gentiles wherever they could gather an audience, in the synagogues of Greece and Italy or on the Areopagus in Athens. After Christianity became the favored religion in the Roman Empire, such bishop orators as Gregory of Nazianzus, John Chrysostom, Ambrose, and Augustine preached many times a week to large audiences of new converts eager to learn about their new faith. In the Protestant Reformation, preaching became the central event of the church gathering. The people needed to be taught the story and meaning of the Bible. Luther, Zwingli, Calvin, and others preached many times a week. The First Great Awakening in the mid Eighteenth Century and the Second Great Awakening in the early Nineteenth Century revived and transformed preaching into its modern form. In the view of many preaching theorists, nineteenth-century preaching reached its peak in Charles H. Spurgeon of London. Throughout all these changes, the sermon has remained the central event in Protestant church services.

The Sermon as Entertainment

Allow me to express my concerns with the state of preaching and the sermon today. I am not speaking of every preacher and every sermon but of the general practice of preaching and audience expectations. In the Seventeenth and Eighteenth Centuries, the ideal preacher was highly educated in theology and the Bible and sermons were instructional, almost like academic treatises, read word for word to the congregation. In the Nineteenth and Twentieth Centuries—the age of Dwight Moody, Billy Sunday, and Billy Graham—things turned emotional and church music served as an emotional "warm-up" for the high-energy evangelistic message. Today, it seems that the order has been reversed, with the sermon being a continuation of the music in the sense that the sermon must appeal to sentiment, begin with a clever hook, contain lots of stories, be marked by humorous moments, and be punctuated by pictures and movie clips. And of course, there are a few Scripture quotations sprinkled throughout. In short, sermons need to be entertaining. Definitely not academic, complicated, and instructional.

What do the new audience expectations mean for the preacher and sermon preparation? It means that preachers spend what time they have left after doing their administrative duties searching for hooks, movie clips, pictures, and stories rather than studying the Scriptures and meditating on how they apply to the people and the age. And for all that work, the modern sermon contains little instruction on the true scope and depth of the Christian faith. Nor does it really challenge the deep pagan myths that animate our post-Christian culture.

Something seems to have gone wrong with the church's work of instruction. In my experience, churchgoers today are abysmally *(extremely)* ignorant not only of the meaning of the Bible but even of its storyline. Hence, they become prey for every "new" idea that hits the New York Times bestseller list, the more mystical, speculative, and metaphysical the better. They unknowingly incorporate Gnostic, Buddhist, Islamic, Hindu, and Native American wisdom into their thinking without realizing that many of these ideas contradict the Christian faith at its most fundamental level. It seems to me that they embrace these ideas primarily because they are interesting, exotic, and fit with the current secular culture of inclusion, universality, diversity, tolerance, and individual liberty.

I do not think listening to a twenty-minute uplifting talk on Sunday morning will repair a half-century of neglect. We may have to do something more radical, such as beginning a serious personal study of the Scriptures or gathering in small groups of serious-minded believers to read and discuss the Scriptures. Or, read together and discuss some great Christian writers and astute Christian critics of modern post-Christian culture.

Fellowship

Now we consider the third component of the church gathering, fellowship. I do not know what comes into your mind when you hear the word fellowship. Perhaps you think of a time for coffee, donuts, and conversation before or after the formal worship service. Or perhaps a monthly or quarterly potluck meal after the worship hour. Or even more informally, hallway conversations before worship services begin or after they conclude. These occasions can produce fellowship, but I have something else in mind.

Sharing in Common

The English word "fellowship" translates the Greek word *koinonia,* which can also be translated sharing or participation or communion. The Christian idea of *koinonia* is that of many people sharing in the experience of Jesus Christ and being united with each other by their mutual participation in him. John speaks of personally seeing, hearing, and touching "the word of life." And he wants others also to experience this life:

> We proclaim to you what we have seen and heard, so that you also may have fellowship [*koinonian*] with us. And our fellowship

[*koinonia*] is with the Father and with his Son, Jesus Christ. We write this to make our joy complete. (1 John 1:3–4)

Paul speaks of the Lord's Supper as a participation in the body and blood of Christ and then connects this experience to the unity of the participants:

Is not the cup of thanksgiving for which we give thanks a participation [*koinonia*] in the blood of Christ? And is not the bread that we break a participation [*koinonia*] in the body of Christ? Because there is one loaf, we, who are many, are one body, for we all share the one loaf. (1 Cor 10:16–17)

The church as it is described in the New Testament is a fellowship, a shared life in Christ. Christians often met in small gatherings to eat, pray, study, and worship together. As we can see from Paul's discussions in 1 Corinthians 10 and 11, they shared in the bread and wine in honor of Christ. They knew each other intimately and were supposed to love each other as brothers and sisters. Their meetings were designed to encourage believers to live as Christians in every dimension of their lives. Their unity, love, and holiness served as a witness to Christ. When one of their number began living immorally, they knew about it, took it seriously, and attempted to intervene. If all else failed, they would refuse to allow this immoral person to meet with them (See 1 Cor 5:1–13). That refusal was made simpler because they met in private homes, not public buildings.

The individual's spiritual welfare and the integrity of the community's witness were at stake.

Intimacy Requires Small Groups

In my life as an individual believer and as a church leader, I have rarely found true fellowship in the gatherings of traditional churches. You can meet with several hundred people once or twice a week in a big, stage-focused assembly for years without getting to know anyone intimately. Few people know your struggles, needs, or interests. You may never hear others' individual expressions of faith. Fellowship, sharing, and community take time, and we do not have time to experience real fellowship with hundreds of people. At minimum, then, a traditional church, if it recognizes the need for fellowship, must put a high priority on getting everyone into a small group designed to promote fellowship. However, some people may need to make their small group their primary church gathering and attend a traditional church for other reasons.

I mentioned above the need to intervene in the lives of Christians who are trapped in immorality or other sins. This is almost impossible in a big church, as I discovered as a church leader. Often my fellow leaders and I discovered problems too late to help. Also, it is difficult to confront people with their sins if you do not know them, they do not know that you love them, and you have not invested time in their lives previously. And in our litigious age church leaders are concerned about getting sued for invasion of privacy. All this adds

(argumentative)

up to the secular ethic of "mind your own business." Nothing like life shared in Christ!

Questions for Discussion

1. Discuss the chapter's definition of worship and its application to the two models of worship, (1) a sea of people praising God and (2) a small group sharing in the Lord's Supper, prayer, and praise.

2. Explain the difference between the two models of the sermon explored in the chapter, that is, as instruction and as entertainment (or inspiration). What is your experience of the modern sermon?

3. Why do you agree or disagree with the chapter's argument that the church needs to return to instruction? Explore possibilities about how churches can renew their teaching function.

4. Explain why you agree or disagree with the chapter's argument that the church's need for fellowship cannot be fully met in large, stage-centered gatherings? List and discuss ways churches can achieve the level of fellowship needed to approach the ideal of "a shared life in Christ."

5. What would the church gathering look like, if we designed it for achieving the three purposes of church meetings most effectively: worship, instruction, and fellowship?

6. No Easy Path to Reform

In every age the church takes shape in the world as an association of people, and it borrows models of organization from the surrounding society, modifying them according to its needs.

Historical Models of the Church

In the early days, the church adopted a model that vested general authority in the apostles and elders at Jerusalem and locally in household patrons and elders that presided over churches in particular cities. Sometime during the Second Century, elders became priests and a single bishop asserted rule over each city. After the church became the official religion of the Roman Empire, it began to model itself on the imperial administration. In the East, powerful bishops (or patriarchs) ruled over the main cities—Alexandria, Jerusalem, and Constantinople—and the surrounding districts. In the West, the bishop of Rome began to model himself on the Emperor, aspiring to become the single head of the whole church. The imperial church developed a huge and complicated bureaucracy to administer its spiritual empire.

The Protestant churches of the Reformation adopted a national or city-state model. As I pointed out in the previous section, Protestant churches in the United States still preserve the basic form acquired in the Nineteenth Century. Some denominations adopted a centralized and bureaucratic administrative structure. Others remained a loosely associated family of local congregations. Still others chose some level of centralization between the two.

Contemporary Models of the Church

However they organize themselves formally, at an informal level certain styles characterize most contemporary churches. *(1) The church as a business.* Church leaders, whatever their official titles, administer the affairs of the church in the way chief executive officers and boards of directors administer businesses. Churches have products, marketing strategies, strategic plans, shareholders, customers, and market shares—all by other names, of course. *(2) The church as a school.* Schools have administrators, teachers, classrooms, lectures, and curricula. *(3) The church as a charitable organization.* This type, too, must be organized to receive and distribute goods and services to its target recipients. *(4) The church as a theater.* Theaters need administrators, theater halls, actors, musicians, and directors. *(5) The church as community center.* Community centers

76

offer gathering places for socializing, meetings of various interest groups, and recreation.

Obstacles to Reform

Rhetoric versus Reality

Though these models and styles dominate their everyday operations, churches still use the rhetoric of the kingdom of God, the family, and the body of Christ to give Christian legitimacy to themselves. Apparently, they do not see the irony in this. They do not resemble a family or hold everyone accountable to the ethics of the kingdom. Nor do they work like the body of Christ. And when an individual actually urges churches modeled on businesses, schools, charitable organizations, theaters, or community centers to return to the family or kingdom or the body model of the church, the systemic logic of these models absorbs, overwhelms, and neutralizes all efforts at reform. At work in each of these models is an irresistible logic fundamentally at odds with the essential nature and mission of the church. All species of starfish can regrow a lost limb as long as the central disk remains, and a few species can regrow the central disk and all other limbs from just one limb. I learned from experience that you cannot reform the traditional church by tweaking this or that program or renaming an office or an activity to sound more biblical. It changes nothing to begin calling the church secretary an "office minister." True reform begins with abandoning the foundational logic of alien models and all their outward manifestations. The problem is in the DNA, not in the name.

The Logic of Assimilation

The irresistible logic of such models as businesses, schools, charitable organizations, theaters, and community centers tends to assimilate every association that adopts them to the archetypical form of the model. When churches operate like other institutions in society they place themselves under the ethics, laws, and social expectations applicable to analogous institutions. By law and social custom, our society expects all employers and such public accommodations as theaters, schools, hotels, and restaurants to treat individuals equally regardless of ethnic origin, religion, physical ability, gender, and sexual orientation. This logic seems as compelling to insiders as it does to outsiders.

Until recently, most churches ordained and employed men only as clergy, and even public worship roles open to laypeople were reserved for men. However, with recent changes in public expectations, many people are asking such questions as, "If women can be senators, professors, heads of fortune five hundred companies, actors, singers, world-renowned athletes, and police officers, why can they not become preachers, bishops, and elders, since the church in all other ways operates like businesses, schools, and theaters?" This logic is powerfully working its way through all churches in the Western world. And, just as it will inevitably drive many churches to assimilate to traditional feminism, it will surely drive many churches to assimilate to the contemporary gender identity revolution.

The problem of assimilation to secular norms cannot be solved by stubborn resistance or supine capitulation. It can be dealt with only by repudiating the subversive logic of public accommodations, schools, businesses, and other secular institutions. It is not the church's essential mission to provide the public with employment, places of honor, social services, social acceptability, recreation, social networking, or any other worldly service. I do not think we have yet realized how much freedom to pursue our mission we have already given up in our past accommodations to secular society and how costly our liberation will be—nothing short of death and resurrection.

More Obstacles to Reform

Perhaps by now you are wondering where I am going in my argument. Do I have anything good to say about institutional churches? And if not, what is the alternative? I promise that I will answer both of these questions soon. For now, however, I need to continue my critique of institutional church practices. For we must rid ourselves of the notion that traditional forms of doing church are the only ways of being the church in the world.

The church will face many challenges no matter what form it takes or what means it uses to accomplish its mission. Jesus was persecuted and his message rejected. We can expect no less. The world is never going to welcome the call to repent of its immorality and idolatry. It loves the broad way of self-indulgence and pride. The way of self-denial and self-control exert no attraction for the majority. Holiness holds no appeal and righteousness excites no hunger or thirst. But sometimes the church creates problems it might not otherwise face by the forms it adopts and the means it uses.

Programs that Need Money

I have already spoken about money at some length. However, I want to mention one more problem with money-driven churches. Contemporary churches instinctively institutionalize programs that need money and lots of it. Hence, churches need contributing members and lots of them. This need introduces ambiguity into the church's evangelistic witness. We are tempted to reduce the price of conversion from "repent and believe the good news" (Mark 1:15) and "take up your cross and follow me" (Mark 8:34) to "come and join our nice church." The motto of every successful retail business is, "The customer is always right." If we set up the church so that we need to attract customers and keep them happy, how can we at the same time call them to "count the cost" of following Jesus (Luke 14:15–35)?

Family Friendly Churches

For most of human history every member of the household worked to support the family. For most of that time families could work together in agriculture, home industries, and domestic chores. There were no electronic media, schools, soccer practices, and music lessons. Evening meals were taken together. But the rise of the modern economy brought dramatic changes to family life. Increasingly, since the end of World War II many middle-class children grow up in homes where both parents work in industry and children spend their days in schools, their evenings doing homework, and their weekends in sports activities. Parents expect daycare workers and schools to educate their children while they are at work and coaches to teach them athletic skills in the evenings and on the weekends while parents relax.

On Sundays modern parents expect churches to act like the daycare centers and schools on which they rely during the week. Church leaders respond to this pattern of expectation by providing childcare, age segregated Sunday school classes, and a full range of youth programs. Churches feel pressure to hire children's ministers, youth ministers, young adult ministers, and family life ministers. They build huge complexes to accommodate all these activities. Otherwise, they may lose families to churches that provide them. In the meantime, parents fail to teach their children the faith or spend time with them modeling the Christian life. Are we helping or hurting families by assimilating the church to the pattern of busyness that is the bane of modern family life?

Guest Friendly Churches

Before the nineteenth-century revivals that periodically swept the United States after 1810, church services were not guest friendly or evangelistic in nature. For the most part, they were planned with insiders in mind. After the American Civil War, the Sunday service became a time to "invite your neighbor" to visit. The sermons and other public activities betrayed an awareness that the "unconverted" may be in the audience. The constant presence of outsiders insured that the church could never conduct its meetings in ways designed to build up the church to maturity in Christ. The original purpose of the gathering was forgotten.

Stage-Centered Meeting

In my experience, most contemporary churches are stage centered. People come to watch, listen, and feel. The preachers, readers, worship leaders, musicians, and singers are the center of attention. The church experience becomes performance and entertainment. If the performance is not satisfactory, we go elsewhere. Center stage in the spotlight becomes a place of honor to be sought. The stage replaces the table, the music replaces the Eucharistic meal, and a general feeling of transcendence replaces Christ crucified and risen.

Questions for Discussion

1. Which one of the contemporary models of the church best describes your church experience? Do you find the rhetoric of the church as a family, the body, and the kingdom at odds with the reality?

2. Does the "logic of assimilation," whereby traditionally organized churches absorb and neutralize every effort at reform, make sense to you? Have you seen this logic in action in your church?

3. Discuss the tension between the church's need for money and its obligation to remind prospective converts to count the cost and take faith seriously.

4. Explain why you agree or disagree with the chapter's warnings to family- and guest-friendly and stage-centered churches. Give examples from your own experience.

7. The Point of it All

We are nearing the end of our project of *Rethinking Church*. In the concluding chapter I want to draw the argument together in a few summary points, make some observations, give some advice, and make a proposal.

Summary Points

- The essence of the church is simple and versatile. Where there is genuine faith in Christ, baptism, and meeting to fellowship with the Lord and each other, the church becomes visible.

- The mission of the church is clear and simple. Its task is to witness by word and deed to the reality of Jesus Christ crucified and risen from the dead.

- Most churches, past and present, augment their essential nature and mission with optional features that they view as legitimate means, appropriate to their situation, to manage their affairs and carry out their mission.

- It is vital to distinguish between the simple essence and mission of the church, which must be present in every genuine manifestation of the church, and the additional features that may be helpful at specific times and places.

- To emphasize the distinction between the simple church and the institutional churches that have taken shape over the centuries, I called the latter para-churches.

- Churches need to examine themselves continually to make sure that the once-helpful additional features do not eclipse the essential features.

- Church reform always begins by comparing the existing condition of the church to its God-given essence. Accidental features that obscure the church's essence or distort its mission must be recalibrated to harmonize with the original norm.

My Hope for the Book

I do not think I have unrealistic expectations about the prospects for human perfectibility. I am not offering a blueprint for the perfect church. I believe, however, that it is possible to do better. I have not argued that para-churches are illegitimate and should be abolished. Many people find them life giving, and I would not take that away from them. I hope, however, that the leaders of these churches will take to heart the distinction between the essential features of the church and the nonessential ones and engage in self-examination and reform. Experience in church leadership has taught me that reform of an existing parachurch will not be easy. You may need to start from scratch, and like Paul avoid "building on someone else's foundation" (Rom 15:20).

I embarked on this project in hope of clarifying my own understanding of the church and my relationship to it. I also hoped that others might benefit from thinking along with me. I had in mind especially those believers who find themselves troubled or alienated from institutional churches but have not lost faith in Jesus. They love being with other Christians but are disillusioned with traditional churches. Some of these believers are older and have given much of their lives to church work, as volunteers or as paid clergy. They are tired and a bit cynical. I want them to know that they do not have to choose between unhappily continuing in the traditional church until they die and melting into the secular culture. There are many options for being the church in this world between these two extremes.

I also had in mind younger people, many of whom are not able to hear the gospel message because it gets mixed with "churchy" language and programs. Having spent a lifetime in the church, I understand "Christianese" and even speak it. I can pick up on the slightest biblical allusion. I understand the symbolic rituals enacted in church services and holy tones of "preacher speak." But most young people do not get it, and acquiring a taste for these things is not a prerequisite for becoming a disciple of Jesus.

If there is any virtue the younger generation values, it is "authenticity." If there is anything it hates, it is "inauthenticity." And if there is any institution that reeks of inauthenticity, it is the institutional church. For sure, there is more to the Christian way of life than authenticity, but Jesus was hard on hypocrites and praised the pure in heart. Authenticity is not trendiness but honesty. It is having no gimmicks and playing no tricks. No plastic smiles, fake happiness, or implausible certainty. Jesus said to his disciples as they left to tell the good news to the Judean towns and villages, "Heal the sick, raise the dead, cleanse those who have leprosy, drive out demons. Freely you have received; freely give" (Matt 10:8). Freely! Not a word that comes to mind when I think of most churches.

I want my young friends to experience a community of other believers where they can learn and teach, know love and fellowship, encourage and be encouraged by others, and give and receive strength. I want them to experience the simple, essential church wherein they can be formed into the image of Jesus and become authentic witnesses to the kindness of God embodied in him. They may at some point learn to speak "Christianese," come to appreciate the arcane (mysterious) traditions of the church, and eventually join a parachurch. That may be a good thing. But let's not force them to begin there.

Some Advice

Why I am a Christian and a Professor

I am a professor. As I look back on my life, it seems that this is what I was destined to become. I love to learn and teach. Thinking is a passion and understanding a necessity. I want to know the truth of things, the cause of things, and the order of things. *Everything* is my subject. I do not mean every subject—chemistry, physics, biology, and sociology—although I am interested in all things. I mean everything all together, the whole universe. What does it all mean? Why does it exist, and where is it going? I want to know its deepest secret—to see it, touch it, smell it, and taste it! I want to enter into it, be immersed in it, and raptured by it. That is why I am a Christian and a theologian. The question for me is not "Why seek God?" The question is "Why seek anything else?" Why should I devote my energies to anything but the best, greatest, and most beautiful of things?

I am in no position to judge my abilities as a thinker and teacher, in absolute terms or in comparison to others. However, I am pretty sure that I am better at thinking and communicating than at church planting and administration. So, when I am asked about the practical implications of what I have been arguing, I hesitate to give advice. Each of us has different experiences and finds ourselves in different situations. There is no one-size-fits-all solution. Perhaps I can best help others by reflecting on what the book means for me.

The Concentric Circle Model of Fellowship

I feel a special bond with other Christians. I want to enjoy their company in conversation, prayer, and worship. I want to give and receive, love and be loved, teach and be taught, strengthen and be strengthened. In other words, I love and need the church. There can be only one church because there is only one God, one Lord, one Spirit, one hope, one baptism, and one faith (Eph 4:4–6). But that church is scattered in time and space. We cannot know each and every member by physical proximity. Yet, I believe I have an obligation to establish a relationship to the whole church in every place and every time. And my love for the whole church is one reason it has taken me so long to acknowledge, confront, and think through my concerns with the institutional church.

I now think of my relationship to the universal church as a huge set of concentric circles. We need an inner circle of a few friends with whom we can spend time in intimate fellowship. Without intimate fellowship of this kind we cannot experience true community. This small church is not an adjunct, a recruiting tool for the big church. It is the real thing. It is where we meet the living and breathing, flesh and blood church. It is not an anonymous crowd, an impersonal institution, or a distant clergy. This inner circle can take many forms. However, it must be open to the next circle and the next and so on until we get in touch with the whole church. Why must we do this, and how can we accomplish it?

We need communion with the whole church because God gives gifts, insights, and experiences to every part, everywhere, and in every age. And every part needs what God has given to every other part. Cutting our little group off from the whole is like limping along with one leg, fighting with one arm, or flying with one wing. We will get so focused on our narrow insights and limited experiences that we mistake the part for the whole. Each little church can be a manifestation of the whole church only as long as its circle is open to all other circles.

How can our inner circle commune with the entire set of concentric circles? Perhaps here is a role for the parachurch. Such churches provide places for many little inner circles to gather to hear from each other and from a wider circle of a tradition—Baptist, Church of Christ, Pentecostal, Wesleyan, Lutheran, and Anglican. Additionally, there are other traditions and even wider circles to encounter. To receive God's gifts and insights into the gospel they preserve, we must listen to representatives from these traditions. Different Protestant traditions need to maintain communication with believers from other Protestant traditions—Lutheran, Reformed, Anabaptist. Protestants must listen to Roman Catholic and Orthodox voices and vice versa. Each little circle needs to be informed in some way by the thought and experiences of all the others. And all of the living need to listen to the voices of the dead. In every age certain Christian truths were perceived with great clarity and others were overlooked. Ours is no different. The church needs historians who keep the past alive. It needs theologians who read the Bible and works from every era and every tradition to keep each little group, every parachurch, and every tradition aware of the whole church.

Keep it Simple

A Simple Church

I wish that every Christian was part of a simple, small church. I hesitate to call it a "church" because the image of the institutional church with all its extra features inevitably comes into our minds. I prefer to think of it as the simplest manifestation of the one church. Simple churches must guard their simplicity by limiting themselves as much as possible to the essential features, activities, and mission of the church, which I described in the first chapter in this book. The simple church owns no property, has no employees, and takes no collections. As far as the government is concerned, it does not exist. Its worship is not stage centered, but community centered; and the community centers itself on Christ. It will have leaders and teachers, but everyone gets to participate. It is a family where even the little ones are honored. Everyone knows everyone. It is not a little church with ambitions of becoming a big church. It has no agenda but to love one another and help each other better serve the Lord. It manifests the fullness of the church because in its life Christ and the Spirit are directing our attention to the Father.

The simple church may take many forms in response to circumstances. If necessary, it can be just your family, and in extreme circumstances even you alone. You may be part of many simple churches, for example, in online fellowship with far-flung friends. Your simple church gathering may welcome guests, or it may be reserved for intimate friends. Worship can take many forms. Keep it simple, and do not forget why the church gathers.

Reform Parachurches

I wish, therefore, that institutional churches would recognize their parachurch status and reform themselves to play that role more effectively. Parachurches cannot replace simple churches, but they can facilitate communication and fellowship among them and between them and the universal church. Parachurches can become places where the best teachers from among the small groups and guests from elsewhere can share insights with the larger gathering. And they can facilitate cooperation among believers in projects that cannot be accomplished on a smaller scale. Also, traditional churches, given their social visibility, can become a person's first introduction to Christianity. They can provide some spiritual support for people that are not involved in simple churches. However, parachurches should recognize that they cannot provide the intimate fellowship and mutual encouragement possible in simple churches. Accordingly, I hope these churches will encourage all of their attendees to participate in something like what I call a "simple church."

Conclusion

Did I achieve my goal in writing this book? Did I clarify my relationship to the church and find a way forward? Perhaps I had already come to my conclusions and simply needed to articulate my reasons. Nevertheless, I think I have learned from this process. As you know from reading previous chapters, I was a leader at the heart of an institutional church for nearly twenty-three years. I gave much time and money to its maintenance. Though I experienced much frustration and anxiety, there were also moments of joy and success. I loved the people. But my overall conclusion is that the traditional system of organization and the social expectations associated with it limit how well such institutions can actually manifest the church in the world. Hence, I came to the conclusion that I could no longer serve as a leader in an institutional church. Nor can I be an enthusiastic participant in the parachurch project. I do not want parachurches to disappear, and I do not want to discourage those who benefit from participation in them. I support traditional churches in their role as a second circle bridging simple churches to the universal church. But I can no longer direct huge amounts of time, energy, and money to their maintenance as institutions.

As I said in previous chapters, I am a Christian, a professor, a theologian, and a lover of the church. I have received an amazing education, and as a professor of theology, I have been given time to teach, read, learn, think, and write. I have had experience as a paid minister and as a volunteer church leader. Hence, I feel called to teach what I have learned to as many people as possible in whatever medium I can. As far as my relationship to the church, I participate in a simple church that meets in our house or, when that is not possible, online. This has been one of the most profound and encouraging experiences of my life. But as a teacher of the faith I feel called to serve all believers everywhere, the universal church. I view my ministry as trans-congregational and trans-denominational. Like a traveling evangelist—who travels mostly via the internet and books—I will speak a word of witness to anyone anywhere.

Questions for Discussion

1. Explain why you think this book may be helpful (or not) to its intended audience? Where do you fit in relation to the intended audience?

2. Discuss the concentric circle model of fellowship with the universal church.

3. Explain why you agree or disagree with the way the chapter relates the "simple church" to the

"parachurch." How does this model fit within your experience?

4. How does your experience with church relate to the author's experience?

About the Author

Ron Highfield (PhD, Rice University) is Professor of Religion at Pepperdine University, Malibu, California. He is the author of *Great is the Lord: Theology for the Praise of God* (Eerdmans, 2008), *God, Freedom & Human Dignity: Embracing a God-Centered Identity in a Me-Centered Culture* (Intervarsity Press, 2013), *The Faithful Creator: Affirming Creation in an Age of Anxiety* (Intervarsity Press, 2015), *The New Adam: What the Early Church Can Teach Evangelicals (and Liberals) About the Atonement* (Cascade, 2021), and a contributor to *Four Views on Divine Providence* (Zondervan, 2011).

If you enjoyed this book, please consider leaving an online review. The author would appreciate reading your thoughts.

Visit Dr. Highfield's author page on Amazon at
https://www.amazon.com/Ron-Highfield/e/
B001JS5TK8/

About the Publisher

Sulis International Press publishes select fiction and nonfiction in a variety of genres under four imprints: Riversong Books, Sulis Academic Press, Sulis Press, and Keledei Publications.

For more, visit the website at
https://sulisinternational.com

Subscribe to the newsletter at
https://sulisinternational.com/subscribe/

Follow on social media
https://www.facebook.com/SulisInternational
https://twitter.com/Sulis_Intl
https://www.pinterest.com/Sulis_Intl/
https://www.instagram.com/sulis_international/

Made in the USA
Monee, IL
24 August 2021